Anchor Hoc

Commemorative

Bottles

and Other Collectibles

Philip Hopper

4880 Lower Valley Road, Atglen, PA 19310 USA

Dedication

I would like to dedicate this book to the employees of Anchor Hocking. F
over 90 years they have toiled to make Anchor Hocking one of the forem
glass companies in the world. I, and the countless other glassware collect
around the world, appreciate the dedication, perseverance, artistry, anc
loyalty to the company responsible for the unlimited variety of glasswar
products.

Copyright © 2000 by Philip Hopper.
Library of Congress Catalog Card Number: 99-64552

Designed by Bonnie M. Hensley
Typeset in Humanst521 BT\Souvenir Lt BT

ISBN: 0-7643-1001-1
Printed in China
1 2 3 4

Published by Schiffer Publishing Ltd.
4880 Lower Valley Road
Atglen, PA 19310
Phone: (610) 593-1777; Fax: (610) 593-2002
E-mail: Schifferbk@aol.com
Please visit our web site catalog at
www.schifferbooks.com

In Europe, Schiffer books are distributed by
Bushwood Books
6 Marksbury Avenue Kew Gardens
Surrey TW9 4JF England
Phone: 44 (0)181 392-8585;
Fax: 44 (0)181 392-9876
E-mail: Bushwd@aol.com

This book may be purchased from the publisher.
Include $3.95 for shipping. Please try your bookstore first.
We are interested in hearing from authors with book ideas on related subjects.
You may write for a free printed catalog.

Contents

Acknowledgements

I would like to thank the following people for making this book a real
Foremost, was Paul Stuart who initially sold me the commemorative bo
collection and spent many hours telling me the history behind the commen
rative bottle production. He was the pivotal figure in documenting this imp
tant part of the company's history. I would also like to thank my fiancé Barbı
Birge who not only put up with my constant "babbling" about the bottles, ‹
who also helped me clean the bottles, create a computer spreadsheet to invₑ
tory the collection, and accompanied me on the emotionally and physicₐ
strenuous photo session at Schiffer Publishing. She also tolerated an extreme
large stack of boxes, resembling a glass collector's "shrine," in her house
months prior to the photo session for the book. A special thanks is extended
Lilith Lund who sold me the Damiana Wine bottle which had been a gift to ̶
from her mother. Lilith wanted to share this rare treasure and part of Ancl
Hocking's history with collectors around the world.

Preface

I began collecting Anchor Hocking's Royal Ruby glassware over 25 yeₑ
ago, but it was not until recently that I first discovered commemorative bottӏ
A dear friend and fellow glass collector, Dr. Leonette Walls of Gardendₐ
Alabama, gave me my first commemorative bottle at the Springfield, Ohio f
market in May 1998. Over the next four months I was able to amass the colӏ
tion pictured in this book. In the absence of company records, undoubte
more bottles will surface as time goes on. Most Anchor Hocking glass collecӏ
are not aware of this exciting new field of collecting.

Introduction

ography of Paul Stuart

Paul Stuart started his long career with Anchor Hocking in 1945 when he
s only 16 years old. He worked there for only three or four months then
nt back to school and graduated from Rockbridge High School in 1948. On
May 1948, Paul returned to Anchor Hocking to begin a career that would
thirty-seven years. In 1951 Paul was drafted into the Army in response to
Korean Conflict. He served 19 months in the Army while stationed in Ger-
ny before returning to Anchor Hocking in 1953. Paul was a machinist at
chor Hocking until his retirement in 1985, after 37 years of dedicated ser-
e to the company. His wife Patsy, also worked at Anchor Hocking's Traffic
partment. She was responsible for freight billing and completed 32 years of
hful service when she retired in 1988.

I had the pleasure to first meet Paul in February 1998. Paul shares my
ssion of collecting, documenting, and displaying glassware. It was quickly
vious to me that Paul had a wealth of knowledge about Anchor Hocking
d the entire history of glass production in this country. Much of the infor-
tion about Anchor Hocking was never recorded and printed records are
in number and hard to obtain. Since Paul is infinitely involved with
king glass formers, he can readily determine if Anchor Hocking makes a
rticular piece of glass.
upled with the knowledge
glass batching possessed
David Bates (retired Sep-
nber 1998), I have been
e to verify items as pro-
ced by Anchor Hocking in
absence of written docu-
ntation.

Dated February 1985 -
Location Anchor Hocking
ol crib and machine shop

Paul and Patsy Stuart - Location: Rockbridge OH

Pricing

Undoubtedly, many of the commemorative bottles pictured in the bo
were produced in very limited numbers. There are no accurate records to doc
ment commemorative bottle production, however, sources in the compa
say usually less than 12 bottles were made to honor any specific retiring e
ployee. Retirement bottles were not normally produced for employees w
less than 35 years service to the company. Greater numbers of bottles w
produced for high school graduations, plant performance awards, special co
munity events, or historical events. Many of the bottles used for food preser
tion were never mass produced and may command higher prices. The prici
is based on the type of event pictured on the bottle, the intricacy of the bo
itself (shape, figures pictured, lettering, amount and type of text, etc.), color
glass, and estimated rarity. It is extremely difficult, if not virtually impossible,
place a value on the historical significance of a particular bottle, especia
when only one example of that bottle exists. All prices are for mint bottles fi
from defects, chips, cracks, or other flaws.

Resources Available to Collectors

Collectors today have a great variety of resources available. With the a
vent of the "electronic age," collecting capabilities have been greatly expand
I can honestly state this book would not have been possible without using t
vast resources available, especially on the internet. Below I have listed t

ources collectors can use for locating antiques and glassware, however, real-
this list is not all inclusive.

Internet Resources: Without leaving the comfort of your home or office,
ı can search worldwide for items to add to your collection. Presently, there
both antique dealers and auction services on the internet.

eBay Auction Service: The eBay Auction Service provides a con-
tinually changing source of items. This internet service contains over
1,900,000 items in 371 categories. Internet users can register as both buy-
ers and/or sellers. The majority of the items remain on the "auction block"
for seven days. You can search the auction database for specific items. A
list of items will be presented following the search. For example, you might
want to find a Fire King Jadite vase made by Anchor Hocking. Because the
seller enters the item's description in the database, you often have to an-
ticipate how the item is described. Don't limit the searches. In this case, you
might have to search under jadite, hocking, fireking (no space), fire king
(with the space), or vase to find the item you want.

Internet Antique Malls: There are several internet antique malls I
have found to be extremely useful in locating glassware. Each mall contains numerous individual dealers with items for sale. The malls I used are
listed below:

1. TIAS Mall – (http://www.tias.com/)
2. Collector Online Mall -
(http://www.collectoronline.com/)
3. Facets Mall - (http://www.facets.net/facets/shopindx.htm)
4. Depression Era Glass and China Megashow
(http://www.glassshow.com/)
5. Cyberattic Antiques and Collectibles –
(http://cyberattic.com/)

Glass shows, antique shops and flea markets: All collectors still en-
searching the deep dark crevices of the local antique shops and flea mar-
s. Many of the best "finds" in my personal collection were located in flea
ırkets and "junk" shops. I recently found 55 Early American Prescut Royal
by ashtrays in a salvage shop in Lexington, Kentucky. Most of the dealers in
ss shows have a good working knowledge of glassware, so "real finds" are
t too plentiful.

Periodicals: Both the *Depression Glass Magazine* and *The Daze, Inc.* are
riodicals which will greatly enhance your collecting abilities. Along with the
merous advertisements for glassware, there are informative articles on all
ets of collecting glassware.

Websites: (http://home.swbell.net/rrglass) I have set up a website to convey infor-
ıtion about Anchor Hocking glassware. As time goes on, the information will
expanded to include photographs of rare items, unidentified items, and
ıeral company information.

Word of Mouth: This is one resource so often overlooked. Let oth know what you are looking for. Consider expanding your search by includ friends, relatives, and other collectors. This book could not have been writ without the help of many fellow collectors.

Do not limit your collecting to only one resource. Remember the items y seek are out there . . . . somewhere!

Request for Additional Information

I am always seeking information concerning Anchor Hocking's glassw production. Much of the information about the company is not available i printed format. This book will undoubtedly be updated and it is imperat new information be made available to collectors. If you have any informati pertaining to the former employees pictured on the bottles, the commemo tive bottle production itself, or facts about the pictures or sayings on the co memorative bottles, please contact me at the following address:

Philip L. Hopper
1120 Choctaw Ridge Road
Midwest City, OK 73130
Phone: (405) 732-6624
E-mail: rrglass@swbell.net
Please be patient if you need a response. I am not in the glassware busines
I am a military officer first and a collector the rest of the time. I will make
every effort to provide prompt feedback on you inquiries.

Chapter One

History Of Anchor Hocking

Anchor Hocking first came into existence when Isaac J. Collins and six
nds raised $8,000 to buy the Lancaster Carbon Company when it went
o receivership in 1905. The company's facility was known as the Black Cat
n all the carbon dust. Mr. Collins, a native of Salisbury, Maryland, had been
rking in the decorating department of the Ohio Flint Glass Company when
opportunity arose. Unfortunately, the $8,000 that was raised was not suf-
ent to purchase and operate the new company, so Mr. Collins enlisted the
p of Mr. E. B. Good. With a check for $17,000 provided by Mr. Good, one
lding, two day-tanks, and 50 employees, Mr. Collins was able to begin op-
tions at the Hocking Glass Company.

The company, named for the Hocking River near which the plant was
ated, made and sold approximately $20,000 worth of glassware in the first
r. Production was expanded with the purchase of another day-tank. This
ject was funded by selling $5,000 in stock to Thomas Fulton, who was to
ome the Secretary-Treasurer of Hocking Glass Company. Just when every-
g seemed to be going well, tragedy struck the company in 1924 when the
ck Cat was reduced to ashes by a tremendous fire. Mr. Collins and his asso-
tes were not discouraged. They managed to raise the funding to build what
nown as Plant 1 on top of the ashes of the Black Cat. This facility was
cifically designed for the production of glassware. Later in that same year,
company also purchased controlling interest in the Lancaster Glass Com-
y (later called Plant 2) and the Standard Glass Manufacturing Company
h plants in Bremen and Canal Winchester, Ohio.

The development of a revolutionary machine that pressed glass automati-
ly would save the company when the Great Depression hit. The new ma-
ne raised production rates from 1 item per minute to over 30 items per
ute. When the 1929 stock market crash hit, the company responded by
veloping a 15-mold machine which could produce 90 pieces of blown glass
minute. This allowed the company to sell tumblers "two for a nickel" and
vive the depression when so many other companies vanished.

Hocking Glass Company entered the glass container business in 1931 with
purchase of 50% of the General Glass Company which, in turn, acquired
ner Glass Company of Winchester, Indiana. In 1934, the company devel-
ed the first one-way beer bottle. Anchor Hocking Glass Corporation came
o existence on December 31, 1937 when the Anchor Cap and Closure Cor-
ration and its subsidiaries merged with the Hocking Glass Company. The
chor Cap and Closure Corporation had closure plants in Long Island City,

New York and Toronto, Canada, and glass container plants in Salem, N
Jersey and Connelsville, Pennsylvania.

Anchor Hocking Glass Corporation continued to expand into other ar
of production such as tableware, closure and sealing machinery, and toilet
and cosmetic containers through the expansion of existing facilities and
purchase of Baltimore, Maryland based Carr-Lowry Glass Company and
west coast Maywood Glass. In the 1950s, the corporation established the
search and Development Center in Lancaster, purchased the Tropical G
and Container Company in Jacksonville, Florida, and built a new facilit
San Leandro, California in 1959. In 1962, the company built a new glass c
tainer plant in Houston, Texas while also adding a second unit to the Resea
and Development Center, known as the General Development Laboratory
1963 Zanesville Mold Company in Ohio became an Anchor Hocking Cor
ration subsidiary. The company designed and manufactured mold equipm
for Anchor Hocking.

The word "Glass" was dropped from the company's name in 1969
cause the company had evolved into an international company with an i
nite product list. They had entered the plastic market in 1968 with the acqu
tion of Plastics Incorporated in St. Paul, Minnesota. They continued to expa
their presence in the plastic container market with the construction of a plan
Springdale, Ohio. This plant was designed to produce blown mold plastic c
tainers. Anchor Hocking Corporation entered the lighting field in Septem
1970 with the purchase of Phoenix Glass Company in Monaca, Pennsylvan
They also bought the Taylor, Smith & Taylor Company, located in Ches
West Virginia, to make earthenware, fine stoneware, institutional china dinr
ware, and commemorative collector plates.

Over the years, several changes occurred in the company. Phoenix Gl
Company was destroyed by fire on 15 July 1978, Shenango China (New Cas
Pennsylvania) was purchased in 28 March 1979, Taylor, Smith & Taylor v
sold on 30 September 1981, and on 1 April 1983 the company decided
divest its interest in the Glass Container Division to an affiliate of the Wes
Corporation. The Glass Container Division was to be known as the Anch
Glass Container Corporation with seven manufacturing plants and its office
Lancaster, Ohio.

Anchor Hocking Corporation was acquired by the Newell Corporation
2 July 1987. With this renewed influx of capital, several facilities were
graded and some less profitable facilities were either closed or sold. T
Clarksburg, West Virginia facility was closed in November 1987, Shenan
China was sold on 22 January 1988, and Carr-Lowry Glass was sold on
October 1989. Today, Anchor Hocking enjoys the financial backing and
sources as one of the 18 decentralized Newell Companies that manufact
and market products in four basic markets: housewares, hardware, home f
nishings, and office products. You may recognize such familiar Newell Comp
nies as Intercraft, Levolor Home Fashions, Anchor Hocking Glass, Goody Pro

, Anchor Hocking Specialty Glass, Sanford, Stuart Hall, Newell Home Fur-
ings, Amerock, BerzOmatic, or Lee/Rowan.

pearance of Markings

Many collectors wonder why the word "Anchorglass" does not appear on
es of glassware until 1949. As an example, the beer bottle produced for
ffer Beer Company in 1947 does have the "anchor over H" emblem on
bottom of the bottle, but the word "Anchorglass" is missing. The company
lied for numerous trademark patents throughout its long history. The trade-
k patent for the "anchor over H" emblem was granted in 1938 and the
emark patent for the word "Anchorglass" was granted in 1945. The com-
y began using the "anchor over H" emblem soon after the Hocking Glass
npany merged with the Anchor Cap Company in 1937. At that time, they
lied for the trademark patent. You will notice the patent application states,
e trademark has been continuously used and applied to said goods in
licant's business since June 11, 1938," while the patent for the word
chorglass" does not state the words are already being used.

Patent application for the
words "Anchorglass."

Patent application for the "anchor
over H" emblem.

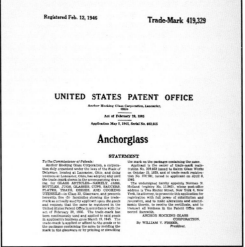

Identification Marks

Over the years Anchor Hocking has used several identification marks mark their glassware. In 1980, the company issued a limited edition 75th ai versary ashtray, pictured below, which portrays the corporate identificat marks. During the photographing, the marks on the ashtray were blacker with a magic marker so they would show up when photographed. Origina when the Hocking Glass Company was established in 1905, the compa used the mark seen on the left side of the ashtray. This mark was used fr 1905 until 1937, when it was replaced by the more familiar anchor ovei mark (center of ashtray) to illustrate the merger of the Hocking Glass Cc pany and the Anchor Cap Company. Finally, in October 1977, the compa adopted a new symbol (right side of the ashtray), an anchor with a mode contemporary appearance to further the new corporate identity.

75th Anniversary ashtray issued by
Anchor Hocking in 1980.

Box for the 75th anniversary ashtray.

Commemorative paperweig
issued to commemorate the
adoption of the new corpo
symbol, the "anchor in a
square" emblem, 2" x 3",
$100-150.

Another commemorative paper-weight issued in Honey Gold, 2" x 3", $100-150.

...rk of Hazel Atlas which is often confused with Anchor Hocking.

...ont Versus Back of the Bottle

In photographing the bottles, we attempted to photograph the most "inter-...ng" side of the bottle. This was not always what was meant to be the front ...he bottle when it was produced. In the captions listed with the photographs, ..."front" is considered to be the side toward the camera and the "back" is ...side away from the camera.

Chapter Two

Retirement Commemorative Bottles

Arnold, H
E.: Front:
E. Arnold
years serv
1933 – 19
Anchor
Hocking.
Connellsv
1933 – 19
Houston 1
1970
*Lancaste
1970 – 19
Picture: Tl
a man pur
on a golf ç
Bottom: T
is an "anc
over H"
emblem, ç
$25-35.

Ball, B.: Front: B. Ball, 45 years, 1929 – 1974, Monongha Glass, Anchor Hocking, Turner Glass, Winc. Lanc. Cnvls. Back: Large "anchor over H" emblem, 5", $40-50.

Barber, George C.: Front: George C. Barber, 1950 – 1982, Chairman & C.E.O. Anchor Hocking. Back: Elaine S. Barber, From your many friends. Picture: none. Bottom: Anchor Hocking Corp., Hand-made, CB, 7 3/4", $40-50.

Bennett, Joseph F.: Front: Good luck "Joe" Hold a big stick & hit a big ball. Back: 1937-19 42 yrs faithful service, Zanesville Mould Co. Picture: On the back is a picture of a golfer hit a ball off the tee, 7 3/4", $25-35.

Boyden, Cora C.: Front: Best wishes for a happy retirement, Cora C. Boyden, cashier – sec., 7-12-35 to 11-1-77. Back: 28 year member of C.C.C (Cora's Conservative Currency). Picture: The front of the bottle has flowers and the back has dollar signs circling a stack of paper money and a bag of coins. Bottom: There is an "anchor over H" emblem, Aug. 27, 1977 testimonial, 9 1/8", $30-40.

Brown, Alfred B.: Front: Alfred B. Brown, 12-12-38 to 4-1-82, 44 years service Anchor Hocking. Back: For our long and happy retirement, tanks for your help. Picture: The front has a ndle rocking chair. Bottom: There is an "anchor in the square" emblem, 7 3/4", $25-35.

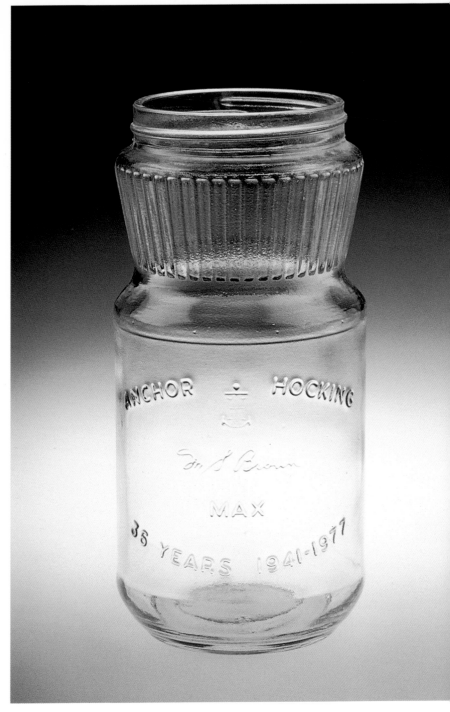

Brown, M. S.: Front: Anchor Hocking, 36 years 1941 – 1977, M.S. Brown Max. Back: No writing. Picture: "Anchor over H" emblem on the front of the bottle. Bottom: There is an "anchor over H" emblem, 7 7/8", $20-30.

Retirement bottle for Max S. Brown. You will notice the sides are deformed when the bottle was handled while the glass was still hot, 7 7/8", $20-30.

Carlisle, George C.: Front: Anchor Hocking Corp., George C. Carlisle, "36" years 2-13-1946 to 3-31-1982. Back: The best *!-&?!!- tank man around. Picture: here are two Anchor Hocking emblems the back. Bottom: There is an "anchor in the square" emblem, 6 3/4", $30-40.

Charlesworth, David H.: Front: David H. Charlesworth, April 10, 1950 to Jan 1, 1981, 3 years service Anchor Hocking Corporation. Back: Best wishes for a long and happy retirement. Picture: The front has a golfer taking a swing, 8 3/8", $25-35.

Cinelli, Aldo P.: Front: "Murph" Aldo P. Cinelli, 1943 – 1975, relief operator. Back: Right glove. Pictures: There is a man in a reclining chair on the front and the right hand glove on the back. The bottom edge of the bottle states: DISPOSE OF PROPERLY, NO DEPOSIT NO RETURN with the "anchor over H" emblem, 6", $25-35.

...way, Charlie et. al.: Front: Cold End Anchor Hocking Corp., Charlie ...onway 35 years, Ed Bond 30 years, ...rt Short 30 years. Back: Winchester ...diana 1982. Pictures: There are two Anchor Hocking emblems and the ...tters GGC on the back of the bottle, 6 3/4", $25-35.

Crispin, Florence: Front: Good luck M‗
C., Mizpah. Back: Florence Crispin, 32
years devoted service to Anchor Hock‗
plant 6, Salem, N.J., Nov. 13, 1939 –
Sept. 1, 1971. Picture: Horseshoe on ‗
front. Bottom: There is an "anchor ov‗
H" emblem, 3 7/8", $20-25.

Darby: Front: Darby, 8-22-59 to 2-1-79,
"anchor over H" emblem. Back: Best
wishes plant 18. Picture: Both the front
and back shoulders have the "Spirit of
'76" and three colonial soldiers, 6",
$20-25.

Deetz, William and Robert: Front: William and Robert Deetz, Bill 42 years, Bob 45 years, combined service 87 years. Back: Lancaster, Ohio, Waukegan, Ill, Salem, NJ, Connellsville, PA, Houston, Tex, Jacksonville, Fla. Picture: There are four small containers on the front, a glass factory on the back with the "anchor over H" emblem, 7 7/8", $20-25.

eMaris, Howard D.: Front: Anchor ocking Corp. Plant 6, Good fishing, appy retirement. Back: Howard D. eMaris "Jake" 8-29-36 to 8-31-79, 43 years service, "A good man to ork for", Salem, N.J. Picture: There man in a boat fishing on the front, 7 5/8", $25-35.

Dembia, E. S.: Front: E.S. Dembia, good
luck to a true friend, 1949 – 1975. Back:
General Foods Kitchens. Picture: None.
Bottom: There is an "anchor over H"
emblem, 6 7/8", $25-35.

Downing, Ward: Front: 1929 – 1975.
There is a small "1971" just under the
lip of the neck. Back: Blank. Bottom:
There is an "anchor over H" emblem,
6 3/8", $20-25.

...esty, Frank G.: Front: Frank G. Ernesty, "Slim", Anchor Hocking Corp. Plant 5 ...nnellsville, PA., Sept. 1, 1935 to July 1, 1978. Back: Quote: "It'll run but not as good" ...im." Picture: None. Bottom: There is an "anchor over H" emblem, 12", $30-40.

Ernesty, Frank G. "Slim." This is a seco
version of his retirement bottle produce
in green glass, 12", $30-40.

Faulkner, Omer: Front: Omer Faulkner,
7-1-56 – 6-29-81, 25 Years Service Anchor
Hocking. Back: For your long and happy
retirement after you refinish it! Picture:
There is a picture of a spindle rocking
chair on the back, 7 5/8", $30-40.

Fauver, Anna: Front: The damned off-ware belt won't run! Back: Anna Fauver, 33 years service, Jan. 17, 1941 to Oct. 1, 1974, Anchor Hocking Corp. Salem, N.J. Picture: An eagle holding a banner with "Good luck repack Annie!" The lower edge of the bottle states: NO DEPOSIT NO RETURN DISPOSE OF PROPERLY with an "anchor over H" emblem, 5 7/8", $45-50.

Fordham, James M.: Front: J.M. Fordham, Vice Pres., 43 years loyal and dedicated vice, May 1, 1929 – Aug 1, 1972. Back: '29 Anchor Cap L.I., – 38 Sched'g. Salem ss, 38 – 44 Asst. Plt. gr. A.H. Salem, 44 – 5 Prod'n. Mgr. Lang. n. Off., 45 - 47 Asst. Plt. Mgr. Winchester, d., 47 – 49 Plt. Mgr. nnellsville, PA., 49 – 56 Plt. Mgr. Salem, ., 56 – 62 Fact. Mgr. anc., O., 62 – 69 V.P. gr., 69 – 72 V.P. Eng. icture: None, 7 1/8", $60-75.

Fordham, John: "Jim" 43 Years 1929 – 1972. Back: New York Sales May 1929 Nov. 1933, Salem, New Jersey Nov. 19 – June 1944, Lancaster, Ohio June 194 Sept. 1945, Winchester, Indiana Sept. 1945 – April 1947, Connellsville, PA. A 1947 – Sept. 1949, Salem, New Jersey Sept. 1949 – July 1956, Lancaster, Ohi July 1956 – June 1972. Picture: "ancho over H" emblem on the front. Bottom: There is an "anchor over H" emblem, 6 3/8", $20-25.

Foster, Eldridge et. al.: Front: Eldridge Foster 31 yrs. 9 mos., William P. Myers 46 yrs. 3 mos., Stanley Woconish 43 yrs. 8 mos., Anchor Hocking Corp., Salem, N.J. Back: no writing. Picture: There is a glass blower on the front of the bottle and the shoulder of the bottle states: DISPOSE OF PROPERLY, NO DEPOSIT*NO RETURN. Bottom: There is an "anchor over H" emblem, 7 3/8", $35-40.

espie, Larry: Front: Larry Gillespie, heroic river rescue. Back: Muskingum River, Zanesville, o, Sept. 14, 1979. Picture: On the front is a picture of a swimmer reaching for a drowning on and on the back there is a picture of a bridge over a river, 7 5/8", $40-50.

Griffin, Shipp: Front: Shipp Griffin. Ba
Salem, Three-o-one. Picture: Three
masted ship on the front of the bottle.
Bottom: Compliments of Anchor Hoc
Corporation, 1776-1976,
7 7/8", $30-40.

Gross, John H.: Front: Best wishes.
Back: 1947 – 1982, John H. Gross.
Picture: The front of the bottle has a
golfer taking a swing. The steel lid on the
bottle has a golf ball with "John Gross
Special" printed on it. Bottom: There are
both the "anchor in the square" and
General Foods emblems, 7 ¼", $40-50.

30

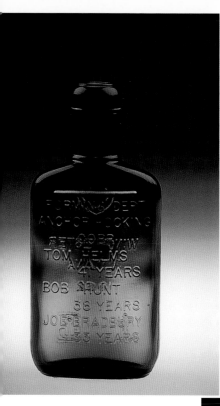

Helms, Tom et. al.: Front: Forming Dept. Anchor Hocking Corp., Tom Helms 41 years, Bob Hunt 38 years, Joe Bradbury 33 years. Back: Winchester, Indiana 1982. Picture: On the back of the bottle are two Anchor Hocking emblems and the letters GGC, 6 5/8", $25-35.

Howard, Arthur: Front: Arthur "Pete" Howard, 50 years, plant 5, Connellsville, 1921 – 1971. Picture: Worker running machine. The lower edge of the bottle states, "KEEP AMERICA BEAUTIFUL – DON'T LITTER, NO DEPOSIT" with an "nchor over H" emblem. Bottom: NOT TO BE REFILLED, 10 1/2", $30-40.

Johnson, R. Elwood: Front: R. Elwood Johnson, "The Judge", Manager – Personnel Services 1942 – 1975. Back: Here Come da Judge. Picture: The back has a picture of a gavel. Bottom: Anchor Hocking Corporation, Salem, N.J., 9 1/8", $50-75.

Kappler and Niss: Front: Fred Kappler, 9-4-34 to 8-31-73, 39 years. Back: Rudy Niss, 1-23-30 to 3-31-73, 43 years. Picture: There are portraits of the two employees with Anchor Hocking Corp. plant 6, Salem, N.J. on the shoulder. Bottom: Salem, New Jersey, 6 3/4", $25-35.

ppler and Niss: This is the other side of the bottle showing Rudy Niss.

Kavanaugh, John J.: Front: Salem, N.J., 1941 – 1973. Back: John J. Kavanaugh. Picture: Shield with Salem High PA Charter Chapter, craftsman of tomorrow, 5 3/4", $25-35.

t, William C.: Front: William C. Kent. Back: 43 yrs. Service. This bottle is to represent
r faithful and dedicated service to Anchor Hocking plant 6, Salem, N.J., Best wishes
n all of us. Picture: "anchor in a square" emblem on the back. Bottom: There is an
chor over H" emblem, 9 1/8", $25-35.

Lawson, E. M.: Side: Vice
Anchor Hocking Corp. 43
years, Feb. 6, 1930 –
June 30, 1973, Excelcius et
Magnus ad Laborum. Bindi
Lawrence, 1930-1973, 43 r
edition, Lang. Ohio. Pictur
"anchor over H" emblem o
side of the bottle, 6", $50-7

Lepley, H. T.: Front: Budgeting time
for fun in the sun. Back: H.F. Lepley,
senior fellow, director, Corp. Bus.
Planning, 38 years service, 8- 4- 41 to
7- 31-79, Winchester* Connellsville*
Salem* Lancaster. Picture: The front
of the bottle has a man reading a
book sitting under a palm tree on the
beach, 7 5/8", $25-35.

Les: There is no last name for this retiree. The bottle states: Les, 40 years, 10-14-29 to 10-14-69, congratulations from plant 18. There is a picture of Les on the bottle and the Pearl emblem repeated four times on the bottle's shoulder. The lower edge states, "NO DEPOSIT*NO RETURN NOT TO BE RE-FILLED", 6 5/8", $20-25.

McCall, Carol: Front: Carol McCall, Senior Fellow 1977. Back: Box shop 4 – 1941, Military 1941 – 1945, Cost ctg. 1945 – 1947, Carton Spec. 1948 1958, Purchasing 1959 – 1982, Total Service 47 years 10 months. Picture: re is an adding machine on the back. om: There is an "anchor in a square" blem and LIQUOR BOTTLE, 8 3/8", $25-30.

McDonald, John R.: Front: Happy retirement! May your greens be smooth and the fairway straight. Back: John R. McDonald, Oct. 1946 – Jan. 1979, 32 years of dedicated service General Food Corp. Picture: There is a golfer making a chip shot. Bottom: There is an "anchor over H" emblem and the picture of a smoker's pipe, 7 5/8", $40-50.

McFee, J. H.: Front: no writing other than the name. Back: Jim McFee, Vice President, 46 years, June 15th 1932 – Feb 1st 1978. Picture: There is a man watching a furnace on the front and three different Anchor Hocking emblems on the back. Bottom: H-8994 LIQUOR BOTTLE with the "anchor over H" emblem, 11 inches to the top of the stopper, $50-75 with stopper.

Bourbon bottle. This bottle was used to design the retirement bottle of Jim McVee, Anchor Hocking vice president. The bottom of the bottle states "LIQUOR BOTTLE", with the mold number H-8994, and the "anchor over H" emblem, 11 inches to the top of the stopper, $10-15 with stopper.

McGinley, Genevieve: Front: July 18, 1927 to Apr. 1, 1976, 49 years service. Back: Good luck Genevieve McGinley. Picture: The front of the bottle has an analytical balance, 6", $35-50.

McVey, Dottie: Front: Dottie McVey, July 17, 1950 to Aug. 1, 1981, 31 years service Anchor Hocking Corporation. Back: Best wishes for a long and happy retirement. Pictures: Female golfer teeing off on the front and the "anchor in a square" emblem on the back, 6 3/4", $20-35.

McWreath, Robert G.: Front: Good luck "Bob", Robert G. McWreath, 1950 to 1978, mould shop forming dept. Back: Best wishes, Anchor Hocking plant 5, Connellsville, PA. Picture: None, 5 ¼", $25-35.

Morrison, Buss: Front: 7th inning stretch. Back: Buss Morrison, Mar. 7, 1923 to
Aug. 4, 1973, 50 years, Anchor Hocking corp. Salem, N.J. Picture: Baseball with crossed
bats on the front. The upper shoulder of the bottle states, "NOT TO BE REFILLED – NO
DEPOSIT*NO RETURN", 5 7/8", $40-50.

Orton, Erby: Front: Need more time Erby Orton. Back: Aug. 15, 1930 - July 1, 1973, 43 years service. Picture: retiree on the front, 6", $20-25.

Polanec, Ed: Front: Ed Polanec, ug. 4, 1952 to Sept. 1, 1982, 30 years service, Anchor Hocking Corporation. ack: Best wishes for a long and happy tirement. Picture: Man sitting in a chair while holding a beer and smoking a cigarette, 6 3/4", $30-35.

Opposite page: Reichard, C
Front: C. J. Reichard, "Clif", 19!
1973, In recognition of your ser
from your west coast friends. Sig
by P.D. Griem.: Back: M. Bake
Brown, D. Egly, M. Hatfield
Jensen, L. Luther, E.F. Mariani
McKenzie, T. Monk, H. Pe
Rainery, C. Schneider, C. Smed
C. Uhrmann, S. Benvenut
Dragoo, K. Griset, T. Humphre
Kirchof, E. D. Mariani L. McCorr
W. Moede, D. Obrecht, A. Perkins
Mullen, A. Scott, P. Thompson
Wilkinson. Pictures: "anchor over
emblem on the front. Bottom: Tl
are the initials "HDN" and "AL
7", $40

Rader, Charlie: Front: Charles "Simmy"
Rader. Back: 37 yrs service, this bottle is
to represent your faithful and dedicated
service to Anchor Hocking plant 6 Salem,
N.J., best wishes from all of us. Picture:
none. Bottom: There is a ½ inch tall
number "37", 5 3/4", $25-35.

Rector, Paul R.: Front: Anchor Hocking
Corp., Paul R. Rector, "48" years, 6-1-34
to 3-31-1982. Back: A career dedicated
to production, sales, & production
planning. Pictures: There are two Anchor
Hocking emblems on the back and the
initials GGC. Bottom: There is an
"anchor in a square" emblem, 6 5/8",
$25-35.

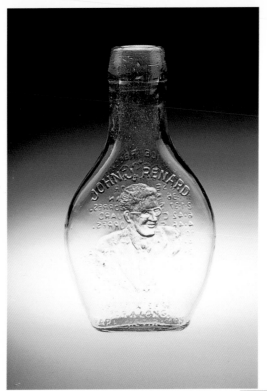

Renard, John J.: Front: John J. Rena
Best wishes for a long, happy retirem
Back: Service record 6-1-36 – 8-31-8
6-1-36 Selector, 11-1-36 Salesman, 2-
Sales Corres., 6-42 Coast Guard, 4-4€
Sales Corres., 10-47 Salesman, 4-57
Sales Mgr., 2-65 Dir. Mkting Serv., 3-€
Mgr. Field Sales, 11-67 V.P. Cont. Div
Mgr. Field Sales, 4-73 V.P. Major Accr
Anchor Hocking. Bottom: There are t
initials "CB" and what appears to be ■
pontil mark, 7 3/8", $50-60.

Savage, Muriel G.: Front: Muriel G.
Savage, 3-17-47 to 9-1-74, Good luck
"Myrt", Twx girl. Back: None. Picture:
On the back of the bottle is a wooden
barrel full of bottles and with the label
Salem Glass 1862, 6 3/4", $20-25.

ll, Herm.: Front: Herm Schell, Best wishes. Back: September 8, 1947, June 30, 1980.
re: There is one large General Foods and one small "anchor over H" emblem on the
, 7 5/8", $30-40.

Shull, Paul P. J.: Front: Paul P. J. Schull
plant 3 Winchester, IN, 5-1-80 to 9-1-
Back: Good luck from all of us at plar
6 1/4", $30-35.

Seagraves, Richard: Front: Richard
Seagraves, Tricky Dick, July 20, 1937
to Jan 1, 1981, 43 years service,
Anchor Hocking Corporation. Back:
Best wishes for a long and happy
retirement. Picture: There is a golfer
taking a swing, 8", $40-50.

nk, H. C. "Bud": Front: Happy retirement Bud, smooth roads, soft landings, best wishes
all of us. Back: H. C. "Bud" Shank, 7-16-1941 to 3-1-1982, 40 years service, 1941 –
loyed plt. 5 C'ville, 1950 – Eng. Dept. Plt. 1 Lang., 1965 – Mgr. Applied Deco. Gen.
Lab., 1980 – Mgr. Process Des. Eng. Center, 12 patents issued. Pictures: There is an
ane on the front and the Anchor Hocking emblem on the back and bottom of the bottle,
3", $60-75.

Spangler, Pea▮
Front: 1941 ▮
Back: Pearl S▮
Spangler, 198▮
42 (+) years,
April 1, 1983
"Anchor Hau▮
Picture: On t▮
back the lady
"buns" have ▮
schredded. B▮
There is an "▮
over H" embl▮
7 1/4", $60-7▮

Spangler, Pearl S.
Back of the
retirement bottle.
Notice the lady's
"buns" have been
schredded.

n, Forest: Front: 1928 Model A Ford. Back: Forest Tobin "Toby", 44 years service 1934
⋅78, Anchor Hocking Gen'l Develop. Lab. Picture: Model A- Ford on the front and two
ᴎor Hocking emblems on the back. Bottom: There is an "anchor over H" emblem, 9",
⋅50.

Towns, Ray: Front: To your future success, Ray Towns, 48 years, Oct. 19, 1925 –
Aug. 1, 1973. Back: Winchester 1925 – 1941, Connellsville 1941 – 1960, Jacksonville 19(
1961, Connellsville 1961 – 1967, Houston 1967 – 1968, Connellsville 1968 – 1973. Bottor
There is an "anchor over H" emblem, 6 3/8", $25-35.

Westenberger, C. L.: Front: C.L. Westenberger A.D. Purch., best wishes to Charlie & Evelyn, 43 years, 1933 – 1976, "anchor over H" emblem. Back: Honest, dedicated, a professional buyer, faithful, fair. A man with balls firm, the man in the arena, 8", $40-50.

hitmore, Franklin E.: Front: Franklin E. itmore,1972 – 1977, Plant 16 Gurnee, , Plt. Mgr. Back: Blank. The bottom of the bottle says "Log Cabin" with the "anchor over H" emblem, 9 5/8", $25-35.

53

Wood, Donald L.: Front: OSU #1 Alumnus. Back: Anchor Hocking Corp., Lancaster, Oh
Memo, To all depts. Subject: Donald G. Wood, Faithful employee account opened Sept.
1937, contract filled Nov. 1978, projected dividends. . . . a very happy retirement, Anchor
Hocking. Picture: There is a football on the front of the bottle. Bottom: There is an "anch
over H" emblem, 9 1/8", $40-50.

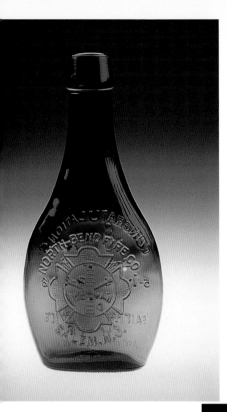

Zane, Bill: Front: North Bend Fire Co, Salem, N.J. Back: Congratulations Bill Zane, 5-13-35 to 12-31-78, 43 years of faithful service, plant 6, Anchor Hocking. Picture: There is an emblem of the North Bend Fire Co. on the front of the bottle. Bottom: There is a 1 inch tall "anchor in a square" emblem, 7 5/8", $35-50.

Zimmer, Robert O.: Front: Good Luck "Bob" Have many good retirement years. Back: Robert O. Zimmer, 1952-1968, 1968-1980, 28 Years faithful service Anchor Hocking Corp., Zanesville Mould Co., "anchor in a square" emblem, 8", $30-40.

Zuk, Alex: Front: Aug. 21, 1961 – Sept. 1, 1981, 20 years faithful service, The Nestle Company, happy retirement Al from your friends, Anchor Hocking. Back: Alex "Pipeline" Zuk. Picture: Golfer taking a swing on the front and the "anchor in a square" emblem on back, 7 5/8", $35-50.

Chapter Three
Anniversaries And Open Houses

10th Anniversary of Plant 4. Front: 1959 – 1969, Plant 4, San Leandro, Calif., tenth anniversary, plant manager – R.J. Brown, P.D. Griem – west coast V.P. Back: M. Baker, E. Brunette, W. Cain, R. French, T. Hankinson, J. Hornik, M. Katreeb, J. McElvogue, A. Nemick, J. Purnell, C. Reichard, L. D. Shouse, E. Smith, T. Thornton, L. Breeland, D. Church, E. Davis, N. Facer, G. Gresh, B.Heller, J. Henry, L. McCormick, H. Kennedy, A. Mladinigh, J. Nolan, H. Pell, V. Putnam, C. Rondi, C. Smedley, R. Steele, L. Young and a banner with the Roman numerals MCMLXIX. Picture: The front has the rising sun, picture of a bridge, the "anchor over H" emblem, and a cable car. Bottom: Anchor Hocking Glass, 7", $40-50.

10th Anniversary of Plant 4. Same bottle but with cobalt glass streaking, 7", $50-75.

50th Anniversary of Salem Co. Memorial Hospital: Front: Founded 1949, dedicated to those who have served our county. Back: Fiftieth anniversary 1969, Salem County Memorial Hospital, Salem, New Jersey. Picture: There is a picture of the hospital on the back and a different building (probably the original hospital) on the front of the bottle. Bottom: Anchor Hocking, plant 6, Salem, NJ, 8 1/8", $50-60.

th Anniversary of American Flint Glass rkers Union. Front: 100th Anniversary, 1878 – 1978, American Flint Glass 'orkers' Union, presented to L.U. 129, ·m, N.J. by Anchor Hocking Corporation plant 6. Back: Salem County, oducing glass for America since 1740, ·s blower and mould bay. Picture: The ·ck of the bottle has a glassblower and ·uld bay and the front of the bottle has ·e union's emblem. Bottom: "anchor in a square" emblem, 7", $40-50.

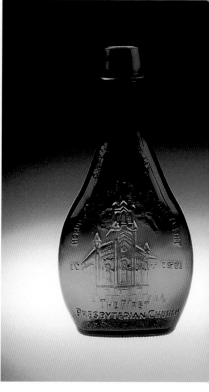

100th Anniversary of Salem High School. Front: 1871 – 1971, Salem Rams. Back: Salem High School. Picture: There is the high school mascot on the front of the bottle and an unidentified emblem on the back of the bottle. Bottom: Commemoration, 100th anniversary, 1871-1971 with the "anchor over H" emblem, 9 1/8", $40-50.

150th Anniversary of First Presbyterian Church. Front: The First Presbyterian Church of Salem, N.J. Back: The orig grant St. Church, 1821 – 1871, 150th anniversary. Picture: There is a pictur the current church on the front and th original church on the back of the bot Bottom: Biblical quote "I am the vine John 15:5, 7 3/4", $50-75.

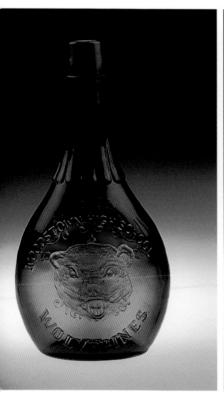

dstown High School. Front: Woodstown
School Wolverines. Back: Class of '51,
ear reunion, 1951 – 1976. Picture: The
of the bottle has the school's mascot.
om: Anchor Hocking Corporation,
m, NJ, 9 1/8", $40-50.

50th Anniversary of Plant 3, Winchester Indiana. Front: Anchor Hocking 50
years, 1931 – 1981, plant 3, Winchester, Ind. Back: E.G. Foust Plant Mgr.,
R.J. Brown Mfg. V.P., L.A. Burnham
Div. V.P. Picture: There is an "anchor in
a square" emblem on the back and
bottom of the bottle, 7", $30-40.

Batch Plant Ground Breaking. Front: Anchor Hocking Corporation, plant 10, May 29, 19
batch plant ground breaking ceremony. Back: None. Picture: There are "anchor over H"
emblems on the front, back, and bottom of the bottle, 10", $40-50.

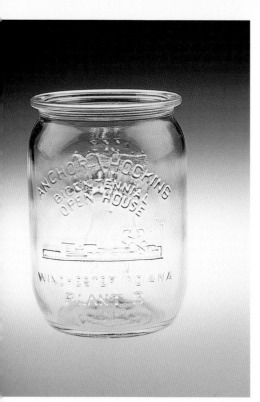

Open House, Plant 3. Front: Anchor Hocking bicentennial open house, Winchester, Indiana, plant 3. Back: 1776 – 1976. Picture: There is a picture of the plant on the front and the liberty bell on the back of the bottle. Bottom: There is a 1 ½ inch tall "anchor over H" emblem, 4 3/8", $40-50.

Carr-Lowry Glass. Front: Carr-Lowrey Glass Company, 1889 – 1976. Back: United States 1776 – 1976, Bicentennial. Picture: There is a picture of the glass plant on the front of the bottle and a glassblower on the back of the bottle. This bottle was made in two colors, 5 3/4", $40-50 each.

Heinz Plant Opening: Front: Congratulations Heinz U.S.A., 100th year, Grand opening o
New Salem plant April 29, 1970, J. Ogden Perry, mgr., Anchor Hocking Corp., Salem, N
Back: The company emblem with "Heinz Tomato Ketchup." Bottom: Mold number H-25
with the "anchor over H" emblem, 8 ½", $40-50.

Open House, Plant 7: Front: Open house 1970, Anchor Hocking Corporation plant 7, Jacksonville, J.A. Biggerstaff Southeast Vice Pres., Forest Lawrence plant manager. Back: Bold new city, Jacksonville, Florida, All American city, Hans Tanzler mayor. Picture: There is a company emblem on the front and the city emblem on the back of the bottle. Bottom: There is an "anchor over H" emblem, 6 7/8", $25-35.

Open House, Plant 7. Closeup of this trial run bottle made for the open house at plant 7 in 1970. You will notice the "J" on the bottle is backwards. All the "J"s on both sides of the bottle were backwards so these should have been destroyed; however, a couple were removed from the plant. They are extremely rare, 6 7/8", $200-250.

Fairfield County Fair: Front: Bicentenni
Thomas Jefferson. Back: Fairfield Cou
Fair, 1850 – 1976, 126 years, create a
new job buy your beverage in a glass
containers, compliments of Anchor
Hocking Container Division, Lancaste
Ohio. Picture: There is a bust of Thom
Jefferson on the front of the bottle. Th
bottle was also made in crystal (not
shown). Bottom: One inch tall "ancho
over H" emblem, 6", $15-20.

Lancaster Lodge #57. Front: Lancaster
Lodge #57 F.&A.M. Lancaster, Ohio.
Back: Sesquicentennial Lancaster Lodge
#57, 1820 – 1970, chartered
Dec. 15, 1820. Picture: There is a
picture of the lodge's emblem on the
front of the bottle, 7 7/8", $35-50.

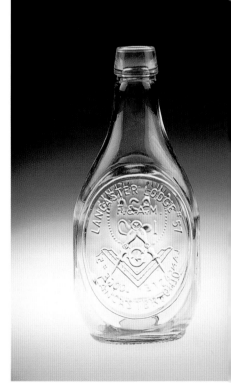

1 House, Plant 5: Front: 1967 Laurel Highlands. Back: Cornellsville Penna 1806. Bottle
)pen house, plant 5, Nov 1967. Pictures: There are pictures of a shooter, water skier,
swimmer on the front and an old furnace on the back. Bottom: Anchor Hocking Glass,
40-50.

New Jersey Tercentenary. Front: New Jersey Tercentenary, 1664 – 1964, people, purpose, progress. Back: Salem oak 1675, Salem, N.J. Picture: There is the events emblem on the front and an oak tree on the back of the bottle. Bottom: Anchor Hocking Glass Corporation, 7", $20-25 each.

New Jersey Tercentenary. Front: Anchor Hocking Corp. Back: Salem Oak 1675, plant 6, Salem, N.J. Picture: There is a ship on the front and an oak tree on the back of the bottle. Bottom: Tercentenary 1664-1964, 3 7/8", $35-50.

Open House, San Jacinto California Front: San Jacinto Open House 1972, Anchor Hocking Corp., plant 18, Houston, Texas. Back: Eighth Wonder of the World, Astrodome, Houston, Texas. "Pitch in, Fight litter." Picture: There is a picture of a monument on the front and the Astrodome on the back, 6 3/8", $30-35.

Open House, Plant 7. Front: Dedication bottle to the employees of plant 7 – Jacksonville, first place in overall plant performance, Container Division, 1980. Back: Anchor Hocking Corporation open house, Dec. 6, 1980, plant 7, Jacksonville, Florida. Picture: There is the "anchor in a square" emblem on the back and bottom of the bottle, 6 3/4", $30-40.

Open House, Plant 18: Front: Open house, June 21-24, 1979. Back: Anchor Hocking Glass Container Division, plant 18, Houston*TX. Picture: There is a long horned steer on the front and the "anchor in a square" emblem on the back of the bottle, 7 3/4", $35-50.

Open House, Plant 18: Front: Open ho June 21-24, 1979. Back: Anchor Hock Glass Container Division, plant 18, Houston*TX. Picture: There is a pictur plant 18 on the front and the "anchor i square" emblem on the back of the bot 7 3/4", $35-50.

ound Breaking, Plant 4. Front: San Leandro California centennial, bi-centennial, '2-1872-1972, home of sunshine and flowers. Back: Anchor Hocking plant 4, plant ansion ground breaking, July 18, 1972. Bottom: There are the initials ALM, 7", $30-40.

Chapter Four

High School
Commemorative Bottles

osite page: Graduation Class of
3, Salem High School. Front: One
try, one constitution, one destiny-
el Webster. Back: Congratulations
school graduates class of 1968,
or Hocking Glass. Picture: There is a
re of a Minuteman intercontinental
tic missile (ICBM) on the front and
anchor over H" emblem on the back
e bottle. Bottom: Salem High

aduation Class of 1969, Woodstown
High School. Front: Apollo 8. Back:
ongratulations high school graduates
lass of 1969, Anchor Hocking Glass,
m, N.J. Picture: There is a picture of
the Apollo 8 emblem with "Borman,
Lovell, Anders" on the front and the
chor over H" emblem on the back of
the bottle. Bottom: Woodstown High
School, 7", $35-45.

Graduation Class of 1970, Salem High
School. Front: One small step for man,
one giant leap for mankind, Apollo 11,
we came in peace for all mankind. Back:
Congratulations high school graduates
class of 1970, Anchor Hocking, Salem,
NJ. Picture: There is a picture of Neal
Armstrong stepping onto the moon on
the front and the "anchor over H"
emblem on the back of the bottle.
Bottom: Salem High School, 7", $35-45.

Opposite page: Winchester Community High School. F
Winchester High School Music Department, golden fal
Back: Winchester High School Athletic Department, go
falcons. Picture: There is a flying falcon on the front and
of the bottle. Bottom: Anchor Hocking, with the "anchor
square" emblem, 6 3/4", $3£

Graduation Class of 1971, Woodstown
High School. Front: The year of reclama-
tion, Anchor Hocking. Back: Congratulations high school graduates class of 1971,
Salem, NJ. Picture: There is a maid
sweeping the floor on the front and the
"anchor over H" emblem on the back of
the bottle. Bottom: Woodstown, 7 5/8",
$35-45.

25th Anniversary. Front: C.H.S. "Coke
class of 1954. Back: C.H.S. 25th anni
sary, 1954 – 1979. Picture: None, 7 5
$40-50.

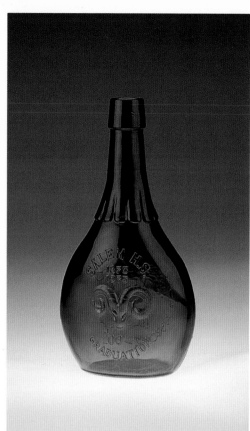

Salem High School 100th Graduation.
Front: Salem H.S., 1875-1975, 100th
graduation. Back: John Fenwick Colony
1675-1975, tercentenary. Bottom: Anch
Hocking Corporation, Salem, N.J., 9 1/
$50-60.

dell Mitchell

Lydell Mitchell's football career started at Salem High School, progressed
e became an All American at Penn State, and culminated with a profes-
al career with the Indianapolis Colts. During his years at Penn State, Lydell
many records. He had his best rushing yardage with 1567 yards and 26
hdowns (career total of 38) during his senior year in 1971. His longest
e run of 71 yards occurred in the game against Maryland in 1969. While
the Indianapolis Colts from 1972 to 1977, he continued his record setting
with a career rushing total of 5,487 yards. His first 1,000 yard season was
975 with 1,193 yards. The commemorative bottle was produced to honor
eat American football hero and All American at Penn State.

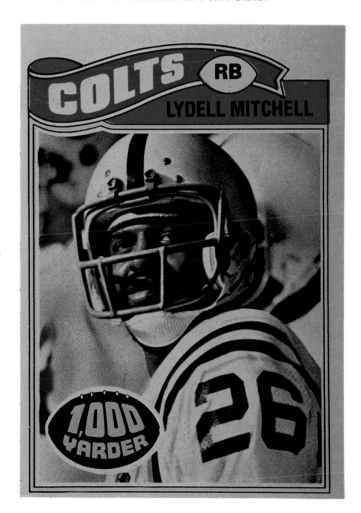

dell Mitchell sports
collector card.

osite page bottom right: Lydell Mitchell. Front: Lydell Mitchell. Back: Lydell Mitchell
American, Salem High 1964-1968, Penn State 1968-1972. Bottom: Anchor Hocking
poration, Salem, N.J., 9 1/8", $80-100.

Ldyell Mitchell sports collector card.

Lydell Mitchell sports collector card.

Chapter Five

Soft Drink Bottles

International Soft Drink Exposition Commemorative bottles: Left to right: flashed royal r\
and crystal 55th, 1973, Miami, Florida; 56th, 1974, Atlantic City, New Jersey; 57th, 1975,
Dallas, Texas; 58th, 1976, Chicago, Illinois; 59th, 1977, Anaheim, California; 60th, 1978,
Atlanta, Georgia; 61st, 1979, Dallas, Texas; 62nd,1980, Chicago Water Tower; 63rd, 1981,
Angeles, California, 7", $20-50 depending upon the year and color of glass.

to right: Brut Great Western 4/5ᵗʰ quart bottle. Bottom: There is an "anchor over H"
lem on the bottom, 12", $1-2; First Decorated Bottle From Plant 3. Front: Commemorative
e, First decorated bottle, May 1, 1979, Anchor Hocking plant 3, Winchester, Ind., Plant
: G. E. Foust. Back: The back of the bottle is the same as the front of the bottle. Bottom:
e is an "anchor in a square" emblem and mold number 51603,
/4", $20-30.

Jacksonville Sesquicentennial. Front: 5ᵗ annual convention, Sept. 24-25, 1972, Jacksonville Florida. Back: Jacksonville Sesquicentennial 1822 – 1972, Anchor Hocking Corporation, Jacksonville, Fla Picture: There is a map of Florida and a soda bottle on the front and an "anchor over H" emblem and the event's symbol the back of the bottle. Bottom: Anchor Hocking Glass, Jacksonville, Fla with an "anchor over H" emblem, 6 7/8", $20-2

American Federation of Labor Convention. Front: This is an Anchorglass one-way bottle, requires no deposit, no return, it's clean and sanitary, imparts no foreign taste or flavor, costs less than cans. Red Top Brewing Co. Cincinnati, Ohio, net contents 12 fl. ozs., internal revenue tax paid. Back: Greetings, American Federation of Labor convention, Cincinnati, Ohio, Nov. 15, 1948. GBBA union made, 100% union made, 100% union packed, 100% union shipped, ask for them, one ways deserve your patronage, compliments of the Glass Bottle Blowers Association. This bottle still has the original contents. NO DEPOSIT NO RETURN NOT TO BE REFILLED is listed on the shoulder of this knurled bottle. Bottom: There is an "anchor over H" emblem, mold number 5865-A, 5 (for plant 5 Connelsville, PA) and 48 (for 1948). The top says "Red Top Beer", 6 7/8", $50-60.

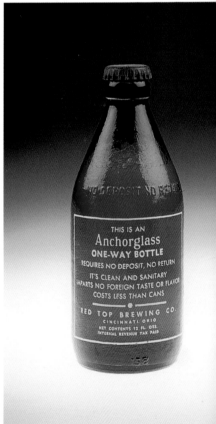

...o right: Coca Cola bottle printed
...ench for sale in Canada, 12 7/
...5-10; 64 oz. Coca Cola bottle
... in 1975, but put into very
...d production because of high
...uction costs and excessive
...t of the bottle (three pounds
...y). This bottle has the date and
...iar "anchor over H" emblem on
...de of the bottle, 13 1/4", $40-
...are 22 kt. gold plated Coca
... Bottle made for the president
...nchor Hocking. The bottom of
...ottle states, "Bethlehem PA,
... mark bottle." There is the
...hor over H" on the bottom,
...4", $200-250, Coca Cola trial
...n Forest Green glass. This bottle,
...lete with the twist off aluminum
...has the "anchor over H"
...em and date of manufacturing
...5) on the side of the bottle,
...4", $100-125.

...Trial run 2-liter Coca Cola bottle
...e in honey gold glass and plastic
...coated. The bottle, mold number
...801, was made in 1977 and has
... "anchor over H" emblem in the
...glass, 12 1/8", $100-125.

Left to right: Plastic coated Coca-Cola bottle, mold number L-64805, has the familiar "anc over H" emblem in the bottom, 11 3/4", $40-50; original trial run bottle with a large Ancho Hocking emblem and the wording, "Trial run, Anchor lite, mark 1-A line, plant five, Nov. 1974." The mold number L-64805 and "anchor over H" emblem are located on the bottom of the bottle, 11 3/4", $75-100.

Trial run Coca-Cola bottle made in 1975 in amber glass. The "anchor over H" emblem is located on the bottom of the bottle. The shoulder of the bottle has NO DEPOSIT NO RETURN, 7 1/4", $100-125.

Trial run Coca-Cola bottle made in amber glass. The bottom of the bottle has Trade Mark Bottle, Kalamazoo, Mich. with an "anchor over H" emblem, 9 3/4", $100-125.

Throw-away Coca-Cola bottle. The bottle was made in 1965 at plant 5 and has the "anchor over H" emblem and NOT TO BE REFILLED on the bottom of the bottle, 7 ¼", $2-4.

I.B.C Root Beer bottle, m number 51603, was mad plant 5 and has the "anc in the square" emblem o the bottom of the bottle, 10 3/4", $2-4.

Fresca bottle in amber glass made at plant 5 in 1969. This bottle has the "anchor over H" emblem and NOT TO BE REFILLED on the bottom of the bottle, 7 3/4", $2-4.

10 oz. com-
morative bottles.
to right: 1776-
6 with the
erican eagle;
er of our country
a portrait of
rge Washington;
Revere's ride
a picture of a
r on a horse;
6 with a picture
drum; Yorktown
1 with a picture
cannon;
cord Minuteman,
heard 'round
world, with a
rait of a minute-
. Bottom:
chor over H"
lem and mold
ber L-6162A,
$5-8 each, $60-
or entire set with
carton.

7-Up commemorative bottles in the original paper carrier.

Chapter Six

Liquor/ Beer Bottles

W & A Gilley:
Commemorative
Anchor FROST bottl
for W & A Gilley Ltd
Winchester, plant 3,
first run, May 1, 198(
The bottom of the
bottle has the "anchc
in a square" emblem
and the words "liquc
bottle." The writing
on the bottle was
done in 22 kt. gold,
12", $40-50.

Liquor bottle made for W & A Gilley Ltd. The bottle holds 200 ml. (6.8 fluid oz.) and has "LIQUOR BOTTLE", the "anchor in a square" emblem, and mold number D-1 on the bottom of the bottle, 6 ½", $2-5.

iquor bottle made for W & A Gilley Ltd. The bottle holds 500 ml. (16.9 oz.) and has "LIQUOR BOTTLE", "anchor in a square" emblem, and d number D-1 on the bottom of the bottle, 8 3/8", $2-5.

4/5 Quart liquor bottle. This portrait bottle states "Federal law forbids sale or re-use of the bottle, 4/5 quart" on the back and mold number R-61, "LIQUOR BOTTLE", 1972, and the "anchor over H" emblem on the bottom of the bottle. This bottle contained Poland Spring Gin distilled and bottled by Lawrence and Co., Inc. of Lewiston, Maine, 10", $5-10.

ate liquor bottle. The back of the bottle states "Federal law forbids sale or re-use of this
e." Picture: There is a picture of a tree on the front and back of the bottle. Bottom: There
"anchor over H" emblem, mold number D-9, and date of 1951 on the bottom of the
e, 9", $10-15.

Rolling Rock beer bottle. The bottle, made in 1969 at plant 5, contained 7 fluid ounces. The mold number 8572 and the "anchor over H" emblem are located on the bottom of the bottle, 7", $2-5.

Robin Hood Ale bottle. The bottle, made in 1972 at plant 5, contained 7 fluid ounces. The mold number L-80709 and "anchor over H" emblem are located on the bottom of the bottle, 6 7/8", $2-5.

Schweppes bottle which contained 10 fluid ounces. The mold number L-61017 and the "anchor over H" emblem are located on the bottom of the bottle, 7 3/4", $2-5.

Damiana Wine bottle, 8 1/2", priceless. Anchor Hocking was contracted to design a wine bottle for the company's new line of "wines for lovers." They wanted the bottles to look li a nude woman, instead wine company officials said the bottles resembled a pregnant woman. This was not the image they wanted to portray, so the design was rejected and th 10 prototype bottles were supposed to be destroyed. An Anchor Hocking employee rescu one of the bottles. This is the only known example of this prototype bottle.

view of the Damiana Wine bottle.

Chapter Seven

Royal Ruby Bottles

Producing the Royal Ruby Color

Many collectors believe all Royal Ruby glass produced by Anchor H
ing was made using gold to give the glass the familiar deep red color. Mar
the pieces made prior to 1950 did contain gold. However, Royal Ruby ʒ
made after that date was made with a glass "batch" mixture containing
muth, tin, and copper. As the "batch formula" was refined, bismuth was el
nated with no effect on the color. When the Royal Ruby glass was first mol
or pressed into shape, it has a very light green color. Once the glass wa:
moved from the molds it was transferred to an annealing oven, called a l
The glass was placed in a lehr and the temperature curve adjusted to re-l
the glass to 1100 degrees Fahrenheit for 15 minutes. The temperature
reduced gradually over the next 1.5 to 2 hours to anneal, or reduce the inte
stresses in the glass. The change from light green to the deep red color, ter
"striking", occurred during the first 15-20 minutes in the lehr. Urea, adde
the original glass batch, acted as a reducing agent and changed the glass f
a light green to a deep red color.

Most collectors of Royal Ruby glassware have noticed extreme color v;
tions. Some pieces actually have clear areas where the reduction process f;
to occur. Three factors effected the "striking" process: temperature, time in
lehr, and the amount of urea in the batch. If the urea level was too low,
glass appeared too light or would not strike. High urea levels caused the r
color to be too dark. Early lehrs were equipped with asbestos curtains to «
trol the temperature in the striking zone of the annealing process. On s«
glasses, the thicker bottom areas and rims actually "struck" during the molc
process. The first Rainflower vase just came out of the mold and has not tur
Royal Ruby. The second Rainflower vase was partially "struck" when molc
Only the thicker portions remained hot enough before annealing to turn re
this vase had been placed in the lehr and allowed to reach 1100 degrees F
enheit for 15-20 minutes, the entire piece would "strike" and would look
the third vase.

Ruby Flashing

A cheaper method of producing Royal Ruby items was to simply coat
piece of glass with a colored lacquer. Even though these are not "true" R«
Ruby, sometimes they are the only way the red color was produced. This
the case for the mold #63-75 whiskey bottle. The bottle was flashed and «
34 made.

The flashing on glass will peel off quite readily. Sometimes it is very difficult [fi]nd pristine flashed items. When I bought a rare ruby flashed Soft Drink [con]vention commemorative bottle recently, the flashing was ruined when the [over]-zealous cashier ripped off the price tag (attached to the bottle with tape). [The] pristine bottle now had a 1 ½" square-shaped ragged clear spot which [dim]inished the bottle's value considerably!

Rainflower vase right after being molded.

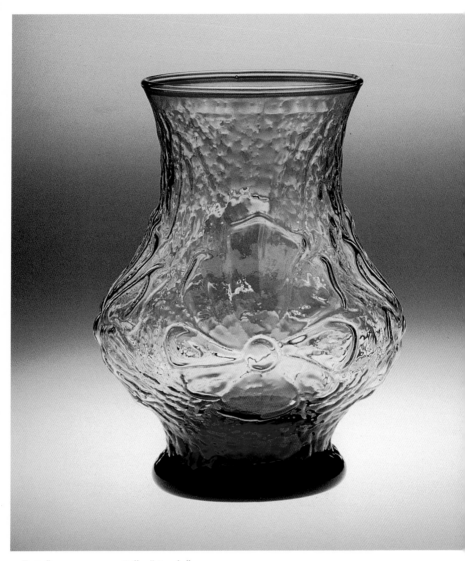

Rainflower vase partially "struck."

flower vase in Royal Ruby.

Ribbed water bottle with a chrome plated band and solid maple wood handle, $250-300

...ed water bottle with a chrome plated band and solid maple wood handle, $35-50. This ...e can be found in crystal with relative ease, but it is rare in Royal Ruby.

Beer bottle made in 1941, mold #8569, $40-50.

Left to right: slim select beer bottle, mold #67-37, $75-80; select beer sample bottle, mold #8589, $100-110. These bottles only differ slightly in the style of the closure. Both bottles were made at plant 5 (Connelsville Pennsylvania) in 1949. There is the familiar "anchor over H" emblem and words "Royal Ruby Anchorglass" on the bottom of both designs.

Beer bottle, mold #61-38, $100-110. This bottle, made in 1949 at plant 5, has a knurled surface and the shoulder states, "NOT TO BE REFILLED – NO DEPOSIT NO RETURN." Knurled bottles have numerous small ridges or bumps on the surface. This bottle was an experimental design produced for Schlitz. Less than 100 of these bottles were produced.

Left to right: export beer bottle with plain surface, mold #63-38A, $100-110; export beer bottle with knurled surface, mold #63-38B, $50-60; export beer bottle with a knurled surface, mold #63-38C, $50-60.

Rare sa|
beer bo|
mold #|
$100-11|
bottle, r|
1947 at|
is not kr|
and the|
shoulder|
"NOT T|
REFILL|
NO DEI|
NO RE1|

seven sizes of juice bottles, made in 1949 or 1950 at plant 5, came in two distinct closure ~~ns~~. One style used a twist off cap while the other used a snap lid. Both versions of the ~~re~~ are seen here. Left to right: mold #50-76A, finish 28-400 (snap cap), 9 ½", $40-50; ~~#50-64A~~, finish 27-870 (screw cap), 8 ½", $40-45; mold #50-51A, finish 28-400 (snap ~~,~~ 7 ¼", $35-40; mold #50-40, finish 27-870 (screw cap), 6 5/8", $35-40; mold #50-28, ~~27-870~~ (screw cap), 5 3/4", $35-40; mold #50-21, finish 27-870 (screw cap), 5 ½", ~~40~~; mold #50-14, finish 27-870 (screw cap), 4 3/4", $15-20.

Closeup of the snap cap for the juice ~~bottles~~. This is called finish #28-400.

Closeup of the screw cap for the juice bottles. This is called finish #27-870.

4/5 Wine bottle, mold #9787-A, 11 ¼", $100-110. This bottle, made in 1950 at p[5, has the familiar "anchor over H" embl[and "Royal Ruby Anchorglass" on the bottom. Around the base of the bottle, "4 QUART" is repeated four times.

Liquor bottle, mold #9783-B, 10", $100-110. This bottle, made in 1950 at plant 5, has the familiar "anchor over H" emblem and "Royal Ruby Anchorglass" on the bottom. Around the base of the bottle, "4/5 QUART" is repeated four times. The shoulder of the bottle states, "FEDERAL LAW FORBIDS SALE OR RE-USE OF THIS BOTTLE."

Squatty beer bottle, mold #63-22, 6 3/4",
$40-50. This bottle, made in 1950 at plant
5, has the familiar "anchor over H"
emblem and "Royal Ruby Anchorglass" on
the bottom. The shoulder of the bottle
states, "NO DEPOSIT NO RETURN – NOT
TO BE REFILLED."

Baby food jar, 3 ½", $25-30. Only "Royal
uby Anchorglass" is written on the bottom
of the bottle.

Chili sa
bottle,
#52-3
$65-75
bottle,
1950 a
has the
"ancho
H" em
and "R
Ruby
Ancho
on the

Ketchup bottle, mold #9547, 8 ¼", $75-85. This bottle, made in 1950 at plant 5, has the familiar "anchor over H" emblem and "Royal Ruby Anchorglass" on the bottom.

Aspirin bottle, mold #82-15A, 4 ½", $15-20. This bottle, made at plant 5, has the familiar "anchor over H" emblem and "Royal Ruby Anchorglass" on the bottom.

Sample beer bottle, mold #B33246-X, 10 ¼", $125-135. This bottle, made in 1963 at plant 5, has the familiar "anchor over H" emblem and "Royal Ruby" on the bottom. The shoulder states, "NOT TO BE REFILLED – NO DEPOSIT*NO RETURN."

Scarce
bottle,
#8580,
$100-1;
bottle,
1947 a
has the
"ancho
emblen
bottom
shoulde
"NOT T
REFILL
DEPOS
RETUR
the bot
the bot
been kr

32 oz. Schlitz Beer bottle, mold #8585C, 9 ½", $75-100. This bottle is extremely hard to find with the original Schlitz labels in place. In fact, this is the only example I have seen in seven years.

Left to right: rare Rolling Rock 7 oz. beer bottle in Royal Ruby, 4 7/8", $250-275; 12 oz. Rolling Rock beer bottle in green, 6", $5-8; 7 oz. Rolling Rock beer bottle in green, 5 1/8" $5-8. The plaster horse in the background was located at a flea market in Ohio.

Whiskey bottle, 7 ½", $150-200. This bottle, made in 1950 at plant 13, has the familiar "anchor over H" emblem and "Royal Ruby Anchorglass" on the bottom. The back of the bottle states, "FEDERAL LAW FORBIDS SALE OR RE-USE OF THIS BOTTLE."

Beer bottle, mold #8565A, 6 3/4", $100-110. This bottle, made in 1949 at plant 5, has the familiar "anchor over H" emblem and "Royal Ruby Anchorglass" on the bottom. The shoulder states, "NOT TO BE REFILLED – NO DEPOSIT NO RETURN." The knurling extends to the top of the bottle.

16 oz. Beer bottle, mold #168-50, 7 3/8", $100-110. This bottle, made in 963 at plant 5, has "Royal Ruby" on the bottom. The shoulder states, "NOT TO BE REFILLED – NO DEPOSIT*NO RETURN."

Mayonnaise jar, mold #10-51, 5 1/8",
$100-125. The bottom of the bottle
has the familiar "anchor over H"
emblem.

Flashed whiskey bottle, mold #63-75,
10 3/4", $100-125. Only 34 of the flashed
bottles were made. This bottle, made in
1954 at plant 5, has the familiar "anchor
over H" emblem on the bottom. The
shoulder states, "NOT TO BE REFILLED –
NO DEPOSIT*NO RETURN."

7 oz. Schlitz beer bottle, mold #67-22, 8", $40-50 with label. This bottle, made in 1950 at plant 5, has the familiar "anchor over H" emblem and "Royal Ruby" on the bottom.

Throw away beer bottle, mold #168-38B, 3/4", $30-40. This bottle, made in 1963 at plant 5, has the familiar "anchor over H" emblem and "Royal Ruby" on the bottom. The shoulder states, "NOT TO BE RE-FILLED – NO DEPOSIT*NO RETURN."

Beer bottle, mold #8568, 6 ¼", $125-135. This bottle, made in 1947 at plant 2, has the familiar "anchor over H" emblem on the bottom. The shoulder states, "NOT TO BE REFILLED – NO DEPOSIT NO RETURN."

at and back view of the rare Owl bank, 7", $250-300. Only about two dozen of these
ks were produced and many of those were damaged when large coins were dropped
the bank causing the bottom to either crack or fall out.

Chapter Eight

Miscellaneous

Perfect Atten
dance. Front
Perfect atten
1973, plant
Back: "Time
never found"
Franklin. Pic
There is a cc
pany embler
the front of t
bottle. Botto
Anchor Hoc
Corp., Salen
7 7/8", $30-

Perfect Attendance. Front: Perfect attendance, 1975 plant 6. Back: "Time lost is never found" Ben Franklin. Picture: There is a company emblem on the front of the bottle. Bottom: Anchor Hocking Corp., Salem, NJ., 7 7/8", $30-40.

Program For Growth. Front: Unity, A.F.G.W.U. - G.B.B.A. Anchor Hocking, keystone to success. Back: Program for growth, Connellsville Pa. Picture: There is a picture of the plant on the back and the union emblem on the front of the bottle. Bottom: There is an "anchor over H" emblem, 6 3/8", $25-35.

gram For Growth. Front: Program for growth, Connellsville Pa. Back: Unity, A.F.G.W.U. -
.B.A. Anchor Hocking, keystone to success. Picture: There is a picture of the plant on the
t and the union emblem on the back of the bottle. Bottom: There is an "anchor over H"
plem, 6 3/8", $25-35.

St. Augustine Florida. Front: Pedro Menendez de Aviles founder, St. Augustine oldest city U.S.A. Back: Spanish, English, Confederate, American, St. Augustine, Fla. Under 4 flags, 1565 – 1965. Picture: There are four flags on the back and a portrait of Pedro Menendez the front of the bottle. Bottom: Anchor Hocking Corp, Jacksonville, Fla. with an "anchor over H" emblem, 6 7/8", $25-35.

N.S.D.A. Convention and Exposition, Houston, Texas, Nov. 15-19, 1971. Bottom: re is an "anchor over H" emblem, 6 3/8", $25-35.

Log Cabin Syrup bottle with 1776 and a picture of a colonial cabin. There is an "anchor over H" emblem on the bottom of the bottle, 8 3/8", $10-15. There are at least 12 differe designs of Log Cabin syrup bottles, however most of the designs do not have the "ancho over H" emblem on the bottom. The Anchor Glass Container Division, a subsidiary of Anchor Hocking Corporation that was sold in 1983, made the majority of the syrup bottl There are also marks from at least two other manufacturers.

Log Cabin Syrup bottle with 1776 and a picture of an American eagle. There is an "anchor over H" emblem on the bottom of the bottle, 8 3/8", $10-15.

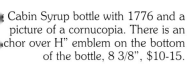

Cabin Syrup bottle with 1776 and a picture of a cornucopia. There is an "chor over H" emblem on the bottom of the bottle, 8 3/8", $10-15.

Log Cabin Syrup bottle with 1776 and a picture of two drummers and a flute player. The is an "anchor over H" emblem on the bottom of the bottle, 8 3/8", $10-15.

Log Cabin Syrup bottle with the Statue of Liberty and the saying "Give me your tired, your poor, your huddled masses." There is an "anchor over H" emblem on the bottom of the bottle, 8 3/8", $10-15.

g Cabin Syrup bottle with a picture of Rushmore. There is an "anchor over emblem on the bottom of the bottle, 8 3/8", $10-15.

Commemorative ashtray which states "38 years of progress, Anchor Hocking Glass Corp 1905-1943", $30-40.

Christmas Commemorative bottles given to the sales representatives. The green is 1978, the crystal is 1981, and the brown is 1982. The bottles state "Happy Holiday from Anchor Hocking." Each bottle has the date and "anchor in the square" emblem on the bottle, 2 5/8", $35-50 each.

American Flint Glass Union bottle. Front: Glass Bottle Blowers Association and American Flint Glass Workers, Local 14 Roy Wynn, Local 203 Daisy Haines, Local 65 Bill Clark, Local 106 Grover Wynn. Back: Mgr. Gene Foust, Mgr. Mfg. Paul Shull, Mgr. Mech. Serv. Ron Turocty, Mgr. Con. Svcs. Bill Voss, Mgr. Ind. Rel. Terry Walter, Mgr. Cust. Serv. Duane Kridle. There is an "anchor in a square" emblem on both sides and bottom of the bottle, 7", $35-40.

ll Samboree 1981. Front: Compliments Seneca Sam's Chapter 24 and Anchor Hocking. Back: Fall Samboree 1981, Muskingum County. There is a picture of neca Sam on the back of the bottle, 8", $35-45.

Opposite page: Sherman, W. T.: F
Standing Stone, Fairfield Heritage Associa
Lancaster, Ohio. Back: General Wr
Sherman, 1820-1891. Picture: There
portrait of General Sherman on the back
Standing Stone Mountain on the front. Bot
There is an "anchor over H" emblem, 6
$4(

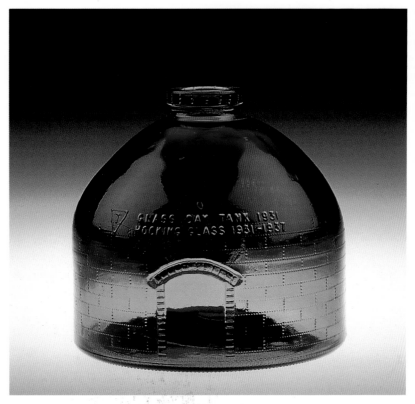

Bottle resembling a glass tank. Front: Glass day tank 1931, Hocking Glass
1931-1937. Back: Anchor Hocking Corporation 1937-1981, plant 3, Winchester Ind, E. G. Foust Plt. Mgr., R. J. Brown V.P. Mfgr., L. A. Burnham Div. V. P.
The bottom of the bottle has the initials of 15 employees, 3 3/4", $35-40.

Bicentennial Peanut Jar. Front: 1776 with an eagle. Back: None. Bottom: There is "anchor over H" emblem, 7", $20-25.

Bicentennial Mason canning jar. Front: Liberty bell, 1776-1976. Back: Mason. Bottom: There is an "anchor over H" emblem, 7", $2-5.

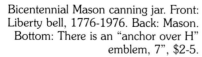

...pened case of Mason home canning ...#1100/46. The package contains eight ...Jars, eight lids, eight rings, and ...uctions for canning, $40-50 per case. ...se commemorative jars also were ...lable in a 1 pint size #1100/45, $40-50 ...case.

Old Glory. Front: 1776 - 1976 with a picture of a pistol and powder horn. Back: Old Glory with a picture of our colonial flag, 5 7/8", $20-25.

Overmyer Mould Company Anniversary bottle. Front: 1920-1970, OMCO 50 years, Pennsylvania - Indiana. Back: Overmyer Mould Company, OMCO 50 years, California - Belgium. This company made molds for Anchor Hocking up until OMCO went out of business in the early 1980s, 12 1/2 inches to the top of the stopper, $450-500 complete w brochure.

Closeup of the stopper of the Overmyer Mould Company anniversary bottle.

There was a small brochure which was suspended from the neck of the Overmyer Mould Company anniversary bottle.

The inscription on the brochure reads; "On our 50th year we at Overmyer take great pleasure in sending to you this decanter in deep appreciation of your friendship over the years. It is our sincere desire to continue to serve your faith in our integrity and your reliance upon our service. We look forward to another 50 years of progress together. Peter L Roesner, President."

1939 World's Fair commemorative bc
Bottom: There is an "anchor over H" emblem, 9 1/8", $5
60 with the label.

Label on the 1939 World's Fair bottle. The label reads: "Pure Cider Vinegar, full strength not less than 5% acidity, contents: 1 quart, Great Atlantic & Pacific Tea Co. packers, New York, NY."

...ntennial B & M Baked Bean jars. Left
...ght: The First American Flag with a
...ure of the colonial flag on the front side
... a picture of Betsy Ross on the back;
...ory - Yorktown 1781 with a horse and
...r on the front side with Valley Forge
...7 with a picture of a colonial soldier on
...back. There are other designs in this
...imemorative series (not shown), 4",
...-15 each.

...year anniversary jar. Front: 50th anniversary. Back: 1933 - 1983, 3 3/4", $3-5. I
have no idea what this jar was meant to
mmemorate. There are no unique events
Anchor Hocking's history that correspond
with these dates.

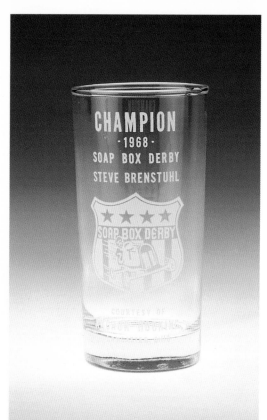

Soap Box Derby commemorative glass. The glass states: "Champion 1968 Soap Box Derby, Steve Brenstuhl, courtesy Anchor Hocking, Lancaster, Ohio", 5", $15-20.

Coal and Coke Museum penny banks. Back: Coal & Coke Museum, charter member, Fayette & Westmoreland Co. of Pennsylvania, 1843 - 1969. Bottom: Officers: J.H. Arnold, Pres., A. Chas. Jacobs, V. Pres., Jos. E. Rulli, Sec., B. F. Husband, Treas., Committee: Paul Sandusky, Jos. M. Driscoll, John B. Shallenberger, Ralph C. Bierlower, Rodney B. Mosier, Rex E. Carter, 4", $50-60 each.

Bicentennial bottle. Front: 1776 - 1976 with a picture of the Liberty Bell. Back: There is a picture of Independence Hall in Philadelphia, PA, 6 7/8", $20-25.

Bicentennial bottle. Front: 1776 - 1976 with a picture of a cannon and ammunion. Back: There is a picture of a colonial soldier and musket, 6 7/8", $20-25.

Christmas bottle. Front: There is a picture
two doves. Back: Season's Greetings Dec
1971, 6 3/8", $30-35.

Commemorative beer bottle. Both sides of
the bottle have two drummers and fife
player with the phrase "spirit of '76" on the
upper shoulder. The lower shoulder states
DISPOSE OF PROPERLY NO DEPOSIT
NO RETURN with a small "anchor over H"
emblem, 6", $20-30.

ısylvania Bicentennial bottle. Front: Bicentennial Pennsylvania 1976 - so your children
tell their children. Back: Fayette Co., Connelsville, So. Connelsville, Indian Creek Valley.
ıre: There is a picture of a family with stars in the background on the front and a map of
ısylvania on the back, 6 3/8", $25-30.

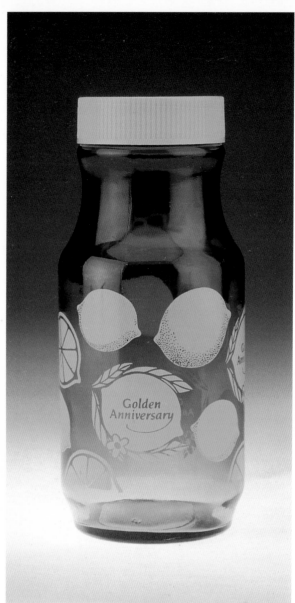

Golden Anniversary: This cont
has lemons all over its surface
plastic lid, and the words "Gol
anniversary." Bottom: There is
"anchor in a square" emblem,
8 3/8", $10-15. I do not know w
this bottle was meant to comme
rate.

Blob of glass given out at the 1969
Ware Coating Seminar held at plant 5,
7" in diameter, $40-50.

144